"This is MY Family

...and that's OK!"

Written by: Isaiah K. Dease
Co Author: Jennifer "Miz J" Primous

This book is dedicated to:
my baby brother Ethan,
my God Parents, Otha & Stasia Mobbs,
my Grandma Gwendolyn Dailey
and the last but not least, my mom Jennifer "Miz J" Primous.

Thank you for supporting me and sharing the greatest memories with
me!

This is my first book and I wanted to write it because I want other children to know that it's ok to not live in a "traditional family". We are all here for a reason and none of us are perfect. I want to encourage grownups to talk to their children about how much they are loved and how important it is to be proud of the family they have.

I hope this book helps kids to open up about their feelings and helps families talk about how important it is to know that they are loved.

This book includes some activates kids can do with their parents/guardians to help start a conversation about love in NON traditional families.

I hope you all enjoy it.

With Love,
Isaiah K. Dease

Hey guys! It's Isaiah here. I'm 11 years old and I'm in the 6th grade. My favorite color is blue. And I like …no wait! I LOVE to play basketball.

My most favorite basketball team is the Golden State Warriors and Stephen Curry is my MOST FAVORITE player … Although, Michael Jordan is the GREATEST basketball player of ALL time!

Some of my friends don't agree, but that's what I like and THAT'S OK! I also LOVE to use emojis what about you? So in this book, you will see a ton of emojis! 😄

Tell me about yourself. What are some of the things you like to do?

What's your favorite color? Do you like to play sports?

I like to make new friends, tell me more about YOU:

My name is

_____

I am _____ years old and in the _____

(grade).

My favorite color is _____

I like to play

_____

A fun fact I would like to share is

_____

_____

Fill in the blanks.

I like to make new friends. It's so nice to meet you!

I live with my mom and we travel as a family. I've visited 11 different states in America and I like to collect postcards to share where I have been.

I was born in Georgia and I've lived in 3 different cities in California .

My mom and I fly a lot. I've visited:

Nevada

Texas

Oklahoma

Arizona

Oregon

Washington

…and sometimes I get to visit my Nanna and Pappa in South Carolina 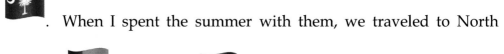. When I spent the summer with them, we traveled to North Carolina and Virginia to see my baby brother Ethan!

My baby brother Ethan is 4 years old and lives with his mom and his big sister. I only get to see my baby brother Ethan when I visit Nanna and Pappa. His favorite thing to do is watch a cartoon TV show called 'Paw Patrol' … he's in love with Paw Patrol. I don't admit it, but when I was his age I liked to watch 'Paw Patrol' too. I think Ethan likes it way more now than I did when I was his age.

I love my baby brother. I help him play and try hard to teach him the right things to do. It's hard work running after him because he likes to get into things and sometimes gets into trouble. Like the time he hid the TV remote control because Nana and Pappa wouldn't let him watch his favorite show for the 5th time in one day. Baby brothers are so funny!

Do you have a brother or sister? Are you older or younger?

Do you live with your siblings? *That's another word for brothers and sisters.*

If you do or if you don't, remember you're all family …and THAT'S OK!

My Nana and Pappa live in a house in South Carolina. They live in a rural city which means there's a lot of trees and farms around them. I love seeing all of the trees and lakes. Their house has a garden in the back yard! My Pappa taught me about planting vegetables and fishing. I remember the summer I helped my Pappa and my Dad in the yard, we took vegetables to my Nana and she cooked them for us to eat for dinner. Eating fresh vegetables from the garden that I picked myself was one of my favorite memories! My Dad has a sister, my Aunt Tia. She lives in New Jersey and has a big dog. My Aunt Tia was a soldier in the United States Military. Although I don't know too many stories about her being a soldier, I am proud to know my Aunt Tia helped to protect our country. During our family reunion, my Aunt Tia and I took a TON of pictures. We all had matching shirts and had a blast making amazing memories.

Who's in your family?

Write the names or draw a picture of your family.

Because I live with my mom and my dad and brother live in different states, we are a <u>NON TRADITIONAL FAMILY</u>! That means, our family is special! Some families have a mom and a son, like mine. Some may have a mom, a brother and sister or a dad and no mom at home. My mom taught me that a non-traditional family doesn't mean anything is wrong or broken but it gives us different ways to share love. Your family may not have a mom or dad. Maybe you live with your grandparents or aunt and uncle. Some families have big sisters living with little sisters and brothers that means they are not your parents but your guardians. Guardians are grownup who take care of kids even if they are not a mom or dad. There are even families who have adopted children and THAT'S OK!

The most important lesson to learn about family is that YOU ARE LOVED. It's hard sometimes, not getting the things I want but when I feel sad, I take the time to write down all of the great things I have and after I read so many good feeling things in my life, I forget about things that I can't change.

My GOOD FEELING LIST is full of the things that make me happy:

1. I have my own room
2. I have a TV in my room
3. MY XBOX ONE
4. My GUITAR (that my uncle gave me)
5. My Stephen Curry Shoes I got for Christmas
6. When my mom cooks my favorite breakfast (OMELETS with meat and cheese)
7. Playing Basketball
8. Hanging out with my friends at the park
9. Playing UNO with my mom
10. Going to the movies
11. Calling my grandma (we laugh a lot)
12. Dancing to the radio in the car
13. Helping my mom cook dinner
14. Spending time with my baby brother Ethan
15. Going fishing with my Pappa and Dad
16. Laughing until my stomach hurts
17. Being silly with my God Mom and God Dad
18. My favorite Golden State Warriors Hoodie
19. Taking Road Trips
20. PIZZA!

There are SO MANY thing I can add to my FEEL GOOD LIST! Anytime I feel sad about something, I start a new one and it helps me feel so much better! You should try it!

WRITE DOWN ALL THE THINGS THAT MAKE YOU FEEL GOOD!

"MY FEEL GOOD LIST"

1. _____

2. _____

3. _____

4. _____

5. _____

6. _____

7. _____

8. _____

9. _____

10. _____

11. _____

12. _____

13. _____

14. _____

15. _____

16. _____

17. _____

18. _____

19. _____

20. _____

WOW?! You have a TON to feel good about! Any time you are feeling sad, Write a NEW LIST and read ALL of the good things you have in life!

My dad and I have a lot in common. We both play instruments ; we both like to dance and be silly. My dad laughs at my jokes even though I know they are silly. My favorite memories with my dad are when we take road trips to Nanna and Pappa's house. We get to talk about a lot of things and he teaches me life lessons. My mom does too, maybe that's just what parents do?

My dad makes his own music! He is a musician and a producer. One day, my dad's music will be played all over the world! My most favorite part about our road trips is listening to his music in the car. My dad's music is better than the music I hear on the radio, in my opinion. I feel special and proud listening to my dad's music knowing that he created it all by himself. He's so cool.

My dad travels a lot too and because we live in different states we mostly talk on the phone. When I'm in California there is a three hour difference in the day. That means we're in different time zones. I live in Pacific Standard Time and he lives in Eastern Standard Time. Sometimes, it's hard to talk to him at bed time because it's even later where he lives. But no matter what, my dad always makes time to answer my calls … and we talk about everything!

What TIME ZONE do you live in?_____ Do you have family that lives in a different time zone? I have a cousin who lives all the way in France 🇫🇷. That's in a different country! I don't know what time it is there right now, but I would sure like to visit someday.

My family has to take a plane to see each other so we don't visit as many times as I want but that's ok. It doesn't change how much we love each other! My mom says we have a love so 💙 BIG, it can't all fit in the same state... and THAT'S OK!

My mom is a writer and a business consultant and does a lot of other things. She is busy and she travels. I am homeschooled so that I can travel with her and still learn all of the things I need to. I get to learn regular school stuff and about how to be a business person at the same time. I don't go to a traditional school, but I still have classes and homework just like any other kid. School is fun for me. Math is my favorite subject. I also like sports. When I grow up I want to be a Sports Announcer on TV!

What is your favorite subject in school?

_____.

My mom is a writer and has a lot of books that she shares to help grownups. I think writing a book is pretty cool. Would you write a book someday? What would you write a book about?

My mom tells me that READING is required to be successful. I read every day. Do you like to read?

I read story books about sports and I like to read books about famous inventors. What are some of your favorite books to read?

Having a family who supports me in everything I like to do feels good and makes me want to be successful to make them proud. I think I want to be a business person like my mom too. She tells me that I can be whatever I want in life if I work hard.

What do you want to be when you grow up?

_____

_____

_____

_____.

Draw a picture of what you think you would look like when you become a grownup:

One of my hero's is Barak Obama. He became the first African American President of the United States of America. He grew up with his mom and dad living in different countries. I watched him on TV talk about how it was hard for him growing up but that didn't stop him from being someone great in WORLD HISTORY!

Some kids grew up without their moms and dads living with them. They were able to live with other family members and sometimes people outside of their family. This means they were <u>adopted.</u> Did you know Steve Jobs, the man known for Apple computers and cell phones, was adopted as a kid? I've learned that many famous people grew up in nontraditional families which means what your family looks like will never change how successful you can be!

Having a family that doesn't live together may seem hard at times but it gives me a chance to travel and visit new places. Besides, to me, normal is so boring.

When I get to visit my Nanna and Pappa, they have a cookout for me

with all of the foods I love! My Pappa is an award winning cook.

He makes the best bar-b-que in South Carolina and he lets me eat as much as I want… What kid wouldn't like that?!

Sometimes I get sad that my dad doesn't live with me. I see others kids playing with their dads and it makes me miss my dad and the fun times we have when we are together. My mom tells me that it is ok to miss my dad. Having those feelings are normal and it's ok to be honest about how I feel. My mom reminds me that it doesn't matter what your family looks like, as long as you are surrounded by LOVE. Your family might look different and there may be some things that are hard to understand, but I've learned to think of ALL the great things about my family and how much I am loved! Even if you are not close to some of your family, you are always connected by love.

My Grandma is my mom's mom. She got married 2 years ago and I was the ring barrier in her wedding! Which means I got to wear a tuxedo for the first time and walk down the aisle while everyone watched me take the ring to her husband Derrick. 💍 I was so nervous because I didn't want to drop the ring. My Grandma wore a long white dressed and looked super pretty. 👰 She cried a lot but I know it was because she was happy. The best part of the wedding was all of the food and music during the party after! We all stayed up late and danced until I was too tired to move. There were so many people at her wedding. There was a big cake and so much food. It was the first time I had ever been to a wedding. I would like to go to another one but without the pressure of being the ring barrier again. That was the best memory with my Grandma even though we have so many, it was a day I remember she never stopped smiling and that makes me happy for her. 💕

My Grandpa Rick is famous and performs around the world with a group called The Blind Boys of Alabama. He is <u>blind</u> which means he can't see but he is a professional drummer and travels around the world singing. How amazing is that?! He won so many awards and even went to the white house to sing for 3 different presidents. He lives in Georgia where I was born and I don't get to see him as much as I would like to either but every time he's in a city near me, we get to go see him perform on stage and I get to go back stage to sit with the band. This year, my mom and I got to spend time in a fancy hotel with my Grandpa Rick. He shared his snacks and I even got to meet the other band members. I am so proud to have a famous Grandpa. Maybe one day I will be a famous musician like him too? Grandpa Rick loves to hear me play guitar and says one day he'll teach me to play the drums like him!

I also have a God Dad and a God mom. <u>God Parents </u>are grownups who help your parents support you in every way. It's like having DOUBLE the love … and double the chores if you get to visit their house. My big cousin Otha is my God Dad and his wife Stasia is my God mom. My mom says they are there to support me just as if they were my mom and dad too! My God Dad and I have a lot in common: we both like to sing loud and make up raps when driving in his truck. He likes to play on his xbox with me and sometimes we like to prank my mom. Like the time he took me on a night trip to the store and we put a stuffed animal under the covers so that my mom would think it was me still in the bed. We laughed so hard when my mom called and told us that she found out I wasn't under the blanket. My God Dad is always joking and I love that he keeps me laughing. My God Mom is silly sometimes too. She was born in Georgia just like me so we like the same foods and like the same music! She is a teacher and she always supports me in my school work. She is very <u>artistic</u> which means she likes to paint, draw and create special crafts. Any time I'm having trouble with my school work, I know I can call on my God Mom to help me figure it out if my mom can't help. My God Parents have a dog named "Gotti" . Whenever I spend time with them, it is my responsibility to help take care of him. Gotti is a small dog with a big personality! He gets dressed up in shirts and hats for the holidays. He even gets his fur styled. My God Parents live in Arizona now, I am excited to visit them for the summer!

I have so many great memories with my family. We all live apart and miss each other sometimes but our love never changes! 💙

I have cousins who live with their mom sometimes and other times they live with their dad. Their mom and dad are <u>divorced</u> which means that they lived together before but now they live apart. I remember my cousin telling me that sometimes they wish their mom and dad still lived together, but they get excited about having two houses 🏠 🏠 to share good memories in. They also love the fact that they get to spend time with their siblings who live with their dad.

My neighbor lives with her aunt, uncle and her little brother. She only gets to see her mom for the holidays. She says that she misses her mom but gets to write her mom letters and gets toys mailed to her every month which makes her feel extra special! 🎁 🎁 🎁

I remember the day my mom planned something EXTRA SPECIAL for me! I was confused, at first, because it was too early in the year for my birthday and no special holidays were coming any time soon. She said she it was time for my "Village Ceremony". I didn't know what that meant until she explained, in our culture, the <u>village</u> is your FAMILY. A group of people, some who are related to you and some who are in the community, who support you when you're growing up. My mom said our Village Ceremony would be really important in my life because it's a time that we all will share our 'Family <u>Covenant</u>'. A Covenant is an agreement or like a contract for a group of people, and my family made an agreement to help me be the best person I can be. 💜💜

At first, I wasn't excited about my village ceremony. It was a lot of work and it seemed like my mom was planning a wedding. She asked her <u>Pastor</u>, who is the leader at my mom's church and a very nice lady, to lead the ceremony. Pastor Fullard let my mom have my ceremony in her private garden in her backyard! It was so big and pretty, she even had a waterfall and all kinds of bright flowers. We invited everyone who was close to me, even my close friends. I didn't like all of the hard work, but I was excited about my mom baking cupcakes 🧁 for me and cooking a special meal, also everyone was going to wear my favorite color blue!

The day of the ceremony was really busy. My mom and my cousins started early in the morning decorating and my God Parents came to our house to get all dressed up. The BEST part about it all was my Dad, Nana, Pappa AND baby brother flew on a plane all the way to California to be with me! It was the best surprise ever! 💕

My friends came, my family was there, my closest friends, some of my mom's friends from the community and even some important community leaders were there. We were all dressed up in blue and white. ✨ My mom and Dad stood up next to me and made a promise to love me and do whatever it takes to make sure I succeed! My God Parents wrote a special letter to me to promise to help my mom and dad. My Grandma, Nana and Pappa even wrote a special promise to me too! I felt so much love around me. There were a lot of grownups crying. My mom says sometimes adults cry when there is an overload of happiness in their heart. 💕 I guess everyone was overloaded because it seemed like a lot of people began to cry. It made me feel more love than I've ever felt before!

Each person stood up and shared how they were proud of me and wanted me to grow up to be a great person. All of the adults gave me gifts and made a promise to look out for me and support me to achieve my goals no matter what. My baby brother just wanted to play with me after, 🤦 but I know that's his way of showing how much he loves me too! 💕

I think every kid should have a village ceremony. 🩶 My mom helps families plan ceremonies so kids will have a special family covenant too! If you had a village ceremony, who would you invite?

Write the names of the people in your village! You can include your friends, teachers maybe even your nice neighbors!

My Village

- _____
- _____
- _____
- _____
- _____
- _____
- _____
- _____
- _____
- _____
- _____

No matter how big or small, your village is filled with all of the people who care about you, who want to support you and will help you reach your goals!

After my ceremony, I wrote thank you letters to everyone who came and shared how much love I felt. Make sure to say THANK YOU to your family for all of the love that they give!

I'm learning, FAMILY means LOVE and no matter what your family looks like, as long as you are surrounded by love that's all that matters! I want you to know that living in a nontraditional family is a good thing and to keep thinking about all of the good things you have in life. Never compare your family to someone else. Everyone's family is just right for them. There are some things in life that we can't control and it may feel hard but remember you are loved and big or small, be proud of the family you have!

You are a very important part of your family and the people who love you will help you be the greatest you that you can be even if they don't live with you. So, remember your family is where you are LOVED. Even if it doesn't look the way you think it should IT'S OK!

Letter from MOM,

In today's society, children are bombarded by subliminal messages of what's considered 'societal norms' when the realities of life are contrary. My desire is to support my son in being open about his truth and I am honored to witness his growth. Like most parents, I was so focused on providing and protecting my son, that I missed opportunities to support him emotionally. I want to encourage all parents/guardians to be open to having a family conversation about the importance of LOVE and what that looks like for you. As a certified Life Coach and working in Social Services, I've learned that children need to be able to express their truths supported by those they trust and depend on the most. No matter how young they are, children have feelings and opinions about the decisions we make for them and if we disregard their emotional wellbeing, we could create an emotional disconnect that could be detrimental as they mature.

We know that we aren't perfect and we all make mistakes, yet I want to take the time to encourage the adults reading this book to be open to hearing how your children feel about their place in your family. The most important part is to first LISTEN without corrections or condemning if their perspectives are different. Simply HEAR them and acknowledge that their feelings matter and support them by being open even if you disagree. As a parent/guardian, remind them that you are doing your best and share with your children that LOVE is the only way you can.

I encourage family therapy for those who have experienced trauma and/or in need of professional support. Contact your local Human Services Agency for guidance and always know: LOVE is the greatest bond.

Here's to FAMILY … no matter what it looks like, YOU are valuable and LOVED!

Sincerely,

"Isaiah's MOM"

Please **Follow/Like/Subscribe** to:

"TRY IT YOU MIGHT LIKE IT"™
@TryIt_YouMight_LikeIt -Instagram

For so much MORE from Isaiah!

THANK YOU for being a part of our extended FAMILY!

Try It You Might Like It, LLC.™
tryityoumightlikeit2018@gmail.com

Made in United States
Orlando, FL
10 February 2023

29767117R00018